50 *majestic* HYMNS

Shawnee Press, Inc.
A Subsidiary of **Music Sales Corporation**
1221 17th Avenue South • Nashville, TN 37212

Visit Shawnee Press online at www.shawneepress.com

Published by:
Shawnee Press, Inc.
1221 17th Ave. South, Nashville, TN 37212

Distribution Center:
Music Sales Corporation
445 Bellvale Road, Chester, NY 10918

Order No. SB1026
ISBN 978-1-59235-177-0
This book © Copyright 2007 Shawnee Press, Inc.

Compiled and edited by Heather Slater
Arranging and engraving supplied by Camden Music
Arrangements by Jane Watkins, Martha Kent, Mark Dickman and Wayne Yankie
Cover design by Chloë Alexander
Printed in U.S.A.

FOREWORD

50 MAJESTIC HYMNS is a rich collection of treasured hymns arranged for piano, voice and guitar. These hymns have been chosen time and again and have endured for generations to become favorites of millions around the world. These great hymns are filled with hope and inspiration, and whether you play them for personal enjoyment or worship with any size group, they will provide endless moments of peace and assurance. 50 MAJESTIC HYMNS brings together a beautiful collection of these timeless treasures which you'll cherish for years to come.

ABIDE WITH ME

Words by Henry Lyte
Music by W.H. Monk

EVENTIDE

1. A - bide with me, fast falls the e - ven - tide;
2. I need Thy pres - ence ev - 'ry pass - ing hour;

(Verse 3 see block lyrics)

the dark - ness deep - ens,
what but Thy grace can

Lord, with me a - bide; when oth - er
foil the temp - ter's power? Who, like Thy -

Verse 3:
I fear no foe, with Thee at hand to bless;
Ills have no weight, and tears no bitterness.
Where is death's sting? Where, grave, Thy victory?
I triumph still, if Thou abide with me.

ALL CREATURES OF OUR GOD AND KING

Traditional
Words by St. Francis of Assisi

With strength and joy ♩ = 76

LASST UNS ERFREUEN

1. All crea-tures of our God and King, Lift up your
2. Thou rush-ing wind that art so strong, Ye clouds that

voice and with us sing Al - le - lu - ia, Al - le -
sail in heav'n a - long, O____ praise Him, Al - le -

-lu - ia! Thou burn-ing sun with gold-en beam,
-lu - ia! Thou ris-ing morn in praise re - joice,

Verse 3:
Thou flowing water, pure and clear,
Make music for thy Lord to hear,
Alleluia, alleluia!
Thou fire so masterful and bright,
That givest man both warmth and light:
O praise Him, O praise Him,
Alleluia, alleluia, alleluia!

Verse 4:
Dear mother earth, who day by day
Unfoldest blessings on our way,
O praise Him, Alleluia!
The flowers and fruits that in thee grow,
Let them His glory also show:
O praise Him, O praise Him,
Alleluia, alleluia, alleluia!

Verse 5:
All you with mercy in your heart,
Forgiving others, take your part,
O sing ye, Alleluia!
Ye who long pain and sorrow bear,
Praise God and on Him cast your care:
O praise Him, O praise Him,
Alleluia, alleluia, alleluia!

ALL GLORY, LAUD AND HONOUR

Words by John M. Neale
Music by Melchior Teschner

SAINT THEODULPH

hon - our to Thee, Re - deem - er, King! To

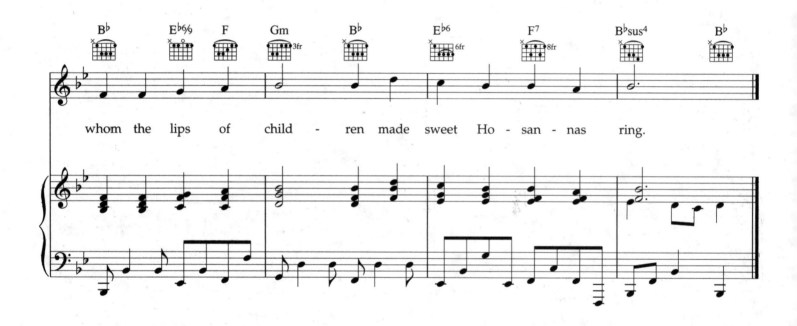

whom the lips of child - ren made sweet Ho - san - nas ring.

Verse 3:
The people of the Hebrews
With palms before Thee went;
Our praise and prayer and anthems
Before Thee we present.
(Refrain)

Verse 4:
To Thee before Thy passion
They sang their hymns of praise;
To Thee, now high exalted,
Our melody we raise.
(Refrain)

Verse 5:
Thou didst accept their praises;
Accept the prayers we bring,
Who in all good delightest,
Thou good and gracious King.
(Refrain)

ALL PEOPLE THAT ON EARTH DO DWELL

Traditional
Words by William Kethe

OLD 100TH

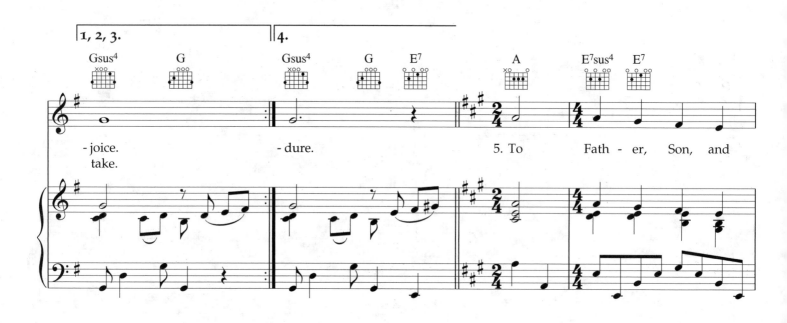

Verse 3:
O enter then His gates with praise,
Approach with joy His courts unto;
Praise, laud, and bless His Name always,
For it is seemly so to do.

Verse 4:
For why? The Lord our God is good,
His mercy is forever sure;
His truth at all times firmly stood,
And shall from age to age endure.

ALL THINGS BRIGHT AND BEAUTIFUL

Words by Cecil Frances Alexander
Music by William Henry Monk

o - pens, each lit - tle bird that sings, He

made their glow - ing col - ours, He made their ti - ny

wings. all. 5. Each lit - tle flower that o - pens, Each

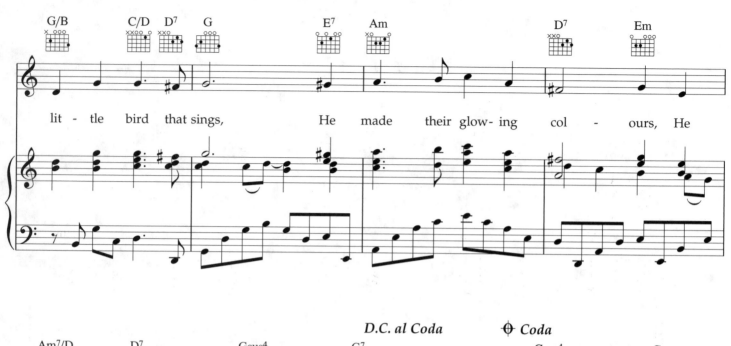

lit - tle bird that sings, He made their glow- ing col - ours, He

D.C. al Coda ⊕ **Coda**

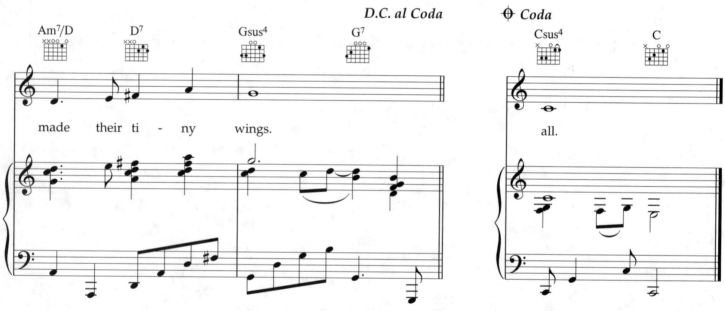

made their ti - ny wings.   all.

Verse 2:
The purple-headed mountain,
The river running by,
The sunset and the morning
That brightens up the sky.
(Refrain)

Verse 3:
The cold wind in the winter,
The pleasant summer sun,
The ripe fruits in the garden,
He made them every one.
(Refrain)

Verse 4:
He gave us eyes to see them,
And lips that we might tell
How great is God Almighty,
Who has made all things well.
(Refrain)

ALLELUIA, SING TO JESUS

Words by William C. Dix
Music by Rowland H. Prichard

HYFRYDOL

With power and majesty ♩ = 94

1. Al - le - lu - ia! sing to Je - sus!
2. Al - le - lu - ia! not as or - phans

His the scep - tre, His the throne;
Are we left in sor - row now;

Al - le - lu - ia! His the tri - umph,
Al - le - lu - ia! He is near us,

Verse 3:
Alleluia! Bread of angels,
Thou on earth our food, our stay!
Alleluia! here the sinful
Flee to You from day to day.
Intercessor, Friend of sinners,
Earth's Redeemer, plead for me,
Where the songs of all the sinless
Sweep across the crystal sea.

AMAZING GRACE

Traditional
Words by John Newton (Verses 1-4) and John Rees (Verse 5)

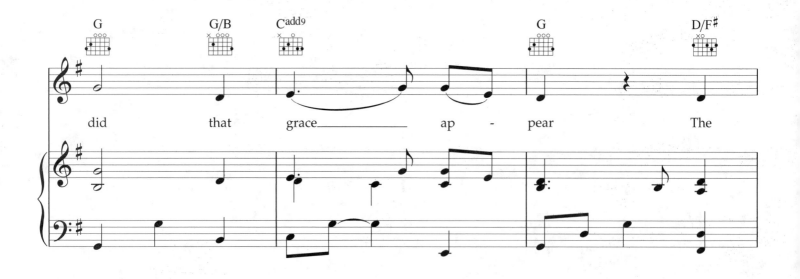

did that grace _____ ap - pear The

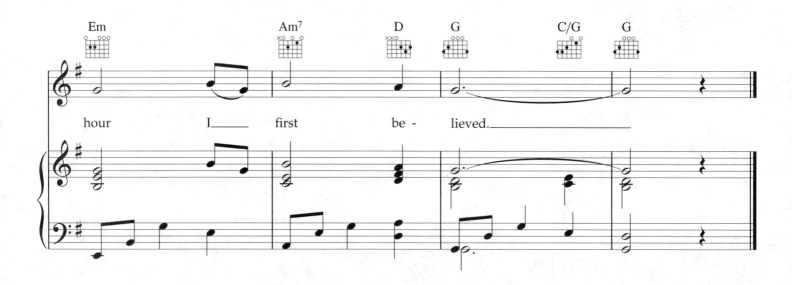

hour I ____ first be - lieved. _____

Verse 3:
Through many dangers, toils, and snares,
I have already come;
'Tis grace hath brought me safe thus far,
And grace will lead me home.

Verse 4:
The Lord has promised good to me,
His word my hope secures;
He will my shield and portion be
As long as life endures.

Verse 5:
When we've been there ten thousand years,
Bright shining as the sun,
We've no less days to sing God's praise
Than when we'd first begun.

AND CAN IT BE

Words by Charles Wesley
Music by Thomas Campbell

pain,   for   me,_____   who   Him_____   to   death   pur -
tries   to   sound____   the   Him   depths____   of   love   div -

- sued?   A -   ma - zing   love!   How____   can____   it____
- ine.   'Tis   mer - cy   all!   Let____   earth____   a -

be,_____   that   Thou,_____   my   God,_____   shouldst   die____   for
- dore,_____   let   an -   gel   minds____   in - quire_____   no

Repeat 5 times

Verse 3:
He left His Father's throne above
So free, so infinite His grace:
Emptied himself of all but love,
And bled for Adam's helpless race:
'Tis mercy all, immense and free,
For O my God, it found out me!
'Tis mercy all, immense and free,
For O my God, it found out me!

Verse 4:
Long my imprisoned spirit lay,
Fast bound in sin and nature's night;
Thine eye diffused a quickening ray:
I woke, the dungeon flamed with light;
My chains fell off, my heart was free,
I rose, went forth, and followed Thee.
My chains fell off, my heart was free,
I rose, went forth, and followed Thee.

Verse 5:
Still the small inward voice I hear,
That whispers all my sins forgiven;
Still the atoning blood is near,
That quenched the wrath of hostile Heaven.
I feel the life His wounds impart;
I feel the Saviour in my heart.
I feel the life His wounds impart;
I feel the Saviour in my heart.

Verse 6:
No condemnation now I dread;
Jesus, and all in Him, is mine;
Alive in Him, my living Head,
And clothed in righteousness divine,
Bold I approach th'eternal throne,
And claim the crown, through Christ my own.
Bold I approach th'eternal throne,
And claim the crown, through Christ my own.

BE THOU MY VISION

Traditional Irish

Flowing ♩ = 86   SLANE

1. Be Thou my___ vi - sion, O___ Lord of my
2. Be Thou my___ wis - dom, be___ Thou my true
(Verses 3, 4 and 5 see block lyrics)

heart, be___ all else but naught to me, save that Thou
word, be___ Thou ev - er with me, and I with Thee

art; be Thou my___ best___ thought in the day and the
Lord; be Thou my___ great___ Fath - er and I Thy true

Verse 3:
Be Thou my breastplate, my sword for the fight,
Be Thou my whole armour, be Thou my true might;
Be Thou my soul's shelter, be Thou my strong tower:
O raise Thou me heavenward, great Power of my power.

Verse 4:
Riches I heed not, nor man's empty praise:
Be Thou mine inheritance now and always;
Be Thou and Thou only the first in my heart;
O Sovereign of heaven, my treasure Thou art.

Verse 5:
High King of heaven, Thou heaven's bright sun,
O grant me its joys after victory is won;
Great Heart of my own heart, whatever befall,
Still be Thou my vision, O Ruler of all.

BLESSED ASSURANCE, JESUS IS MINE

Words by Fanny J. Crosby
Music by Phoebe P. Knapp

Verse 3:
Perfect submission, all is at rest,
I in my Saviour am happy and blest;
Watching and waiting, looking above,
Filled with His goodness, lost in His love.

BREATHE ON ME, BREATH OF GOD

Words by Edwin Hatch
Music by Robert Jackson

TRENTHAM

Thoughtfully ♩ = 90

1. Breathe on me, breath of God,
2. Breathe on me, breath of God,

(Verse 3 see block lyrics)

fill me with life a - new,
un - til my heart is pure,

that I may love what Thou dost
un - til my will is one with

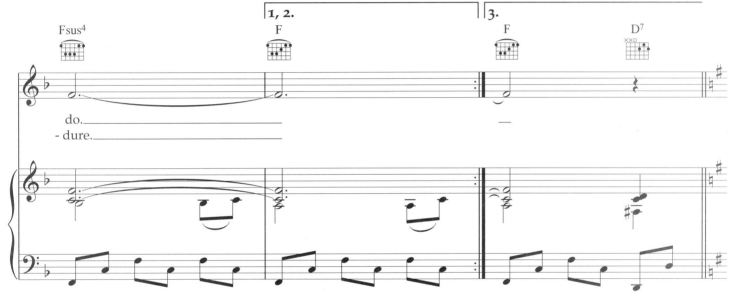

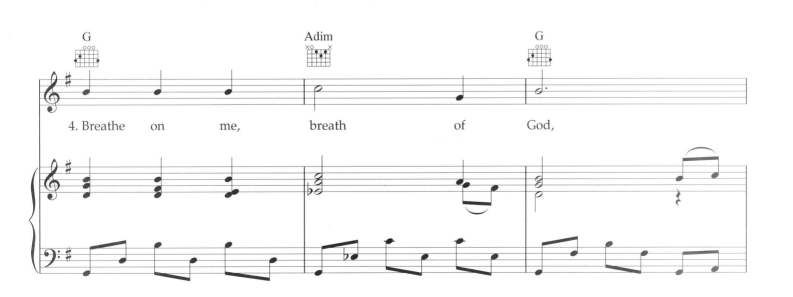

Verse 3:
Breathe on me, breath of God,
Till I am wholly Thine,
Until this earthly part of me
Glows with Thy fire divine.

THE DAY THOU GAVEST

Words by John Ellerton
Music by Clement C. Scholefield

SAINT CLEMENT

With movement ♩ = 88

1. The day___ Thou ga - vest, Lord,___ is
thank___ Thee that___ Thy Church,___ un -

(Verses 3 and 4 see block lyrics)

end - ed, the dark - ness falls___ at Thy be -
sleep - ing while earth rolls on - ward in - to

- hest; to Thee___ our morn - ing hymns___ a -
light, through all___ the world___ her watch___ is

scend - ed, Thy praise___ shall sanc - ti - fy___ our
keep - ing and rests___ not now___ by day___ nor

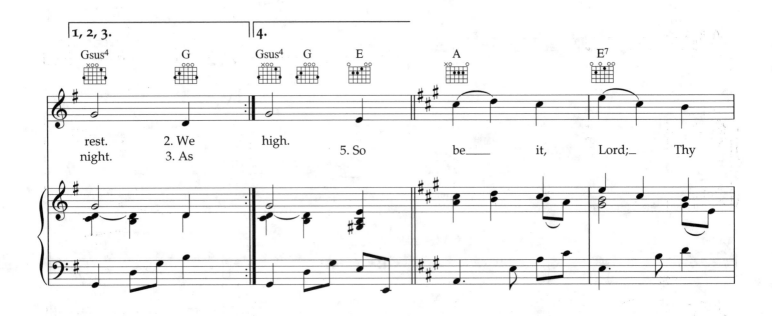

1, 2, 3. | **4.**

rest.   2. We   high.
night.   3. As

5. So   be___ it, Lord;___ Thy

throne__ shall nev - er like earth's proud em - pires,

Verse 3:
As o'er each continent and island
The dawn leads on another day,
The voice of prayer is never silent,
Nor dies the strain of praise away.

Verse 4:
The sun that bids us rest is waking
Our brethren 'neath the western sky,
And hour by hour fresh lips are making
Thy wondrous doings heard on high.

CHRIST IS MADE THE SURE FOUNDATION

English translation by John Mason Neale
Music by Henry Purcell

WESTMINSTER ABBEY

1. Christ is made the sure foun - da - tion,
2. All that de - di - ca - ted ci - ty,

(Verses 3, 4 and 5 see block lyrics)

Christ the head and cor - ner - stone,
dear - ly loved of God on high,

cho - sen of the Lord, and pre - cious,
in ex - ul - tant ju - bi - la - tion

Verse 3:
To this temple, where we call Thee,
Come, O Lord of Hosts, today;
With Thy wonted loving-kindness
Hear Thy servants as they pray,
And Thy fullest benediction
Shed within its walls alway.

Verse 4:
Here vouchsafe to all Thy servants
What they ask of Thee to gain;
What they gain from Thee, forever
With the blessèd to retain,
And hereafter in Thy glory
Evermore with Thee to reign.

Verse 5:
Laud and honour to the Father,
Laud and honour to the Son,
Laud and honour to the Spirit,
Ever Three, and ever One,
Consubstantial, co-eternal,
While unending ages run.

THE CHURCH'S ONE FOUNDATION

Words by Samuel John Stone
Music by Samuel Sebastian Wesley

AURELIA

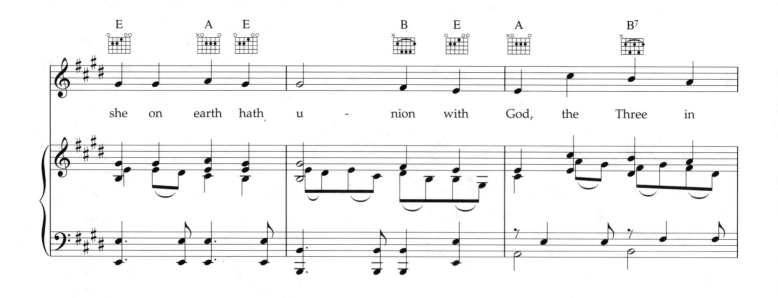

she on earth hath u - nion with God, the Three in

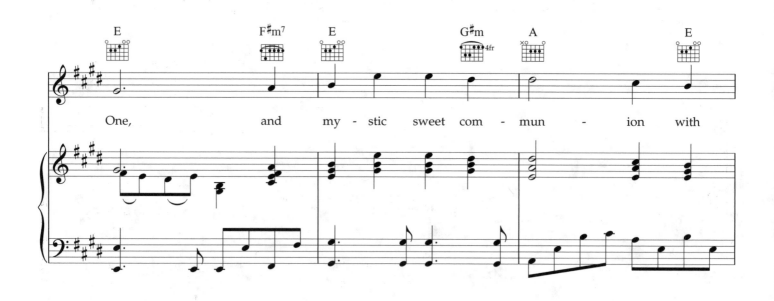

One, and my - stic sweet com - mun - ion with

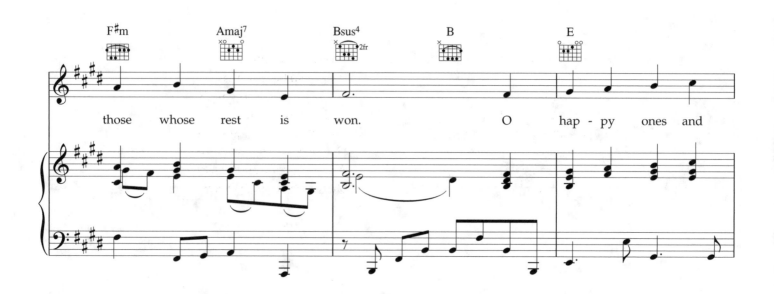

those whose rest is won. O hap - py ones and

Verse 3:
Though with a scornful wonder
Men see her sore oppressed,
By schisms rent asunder,
By heresies distressed;
Yet saints their watch are keeping,
Their cry goes up, "How long?"
And soon the night of weeping
Shall be the morn of song.

Verse 4:
'Mid toil and tribulation,
And tumult of her war,
She waits the consummation
Of peace for evermore;
Till with the vision glorious
Her longing eyes are blessed,
And the great Church victorious
Shall be the Church at rest.

CROWN HIM WITH MANY CROWNS

Words by Matthew Bridges
Music by George J. Elvey

With majesty and power ♩ = 100

DIADEMATA

1. Crown Him with ma - ny crowns, The Lamb up - on His
2. Crown Him the Vir - gin's Son: The God in - car - nate

with pedal

throne: Hark! how the heav'n - ly an - them drowns All
born, Whose arm the crim - son tro - phies won Which

mu - sic but its own! A - wake, my soul, and
now his brow a - dorn; Fruit of the mys - tic

cresc.

Verse 3:
Crown Him the Lord of love,
Behold His hands and side,
Rich wounds, yet visible above,
In beauty glorified.
No angel in the sky
Can fully bear that sight,
But downward bends each burning eye
At mysteries so bright.

Verse 4:
Crown Him the Lord of years,
The Potentate of time,
Creator of the rolling spheres,
Ineffably sublime.
All hail, Redeemer, hail!
For Thou has died for me;
Thy praise and glory shall not fail
Throughout eternity.

DEAR LORD AND FATHER OF MANKIND

Words by John Greenleaf Whittier
Music by Hubert H. Parry

flesh re-tire; speak through the earth-quake, wind and fire, O still, small voice of calm; O still, small voice of calm.

Verse 3:
O Sabbath rest by Galilee!
O calm of hills above,
Where Jesus knelt to share with Thee
The silence of eternity
Interpreted by love!
Interpreted by love!

Verse 4:
Drop Thy still dews of quietness,
Till all our strivings cease;
Take from our souls the strain and stress,
And let our ordered lives confess
The beauty of Thy peace;
The beauty of Thy peace.

ETERNAL FATHER, STRONG TO SAVE

Words by William Whiting
Music by John Bacchus Dykes

MELITA

Verse 3:
O sacred Spirit, Who didst brood
Upon the waters dark and rude,
And bid their angry tumult cease,
And give, for wild confusion, peace:
O hear us when we cry to Thee
For those in peril on the sea.

FOR THE BEAUTY OF THE EARTH

Words by Folliot S. Pierpoint
Music by Conrad Kocher and William H. Monk

Flowing, with joy ♩ = 100

DIX

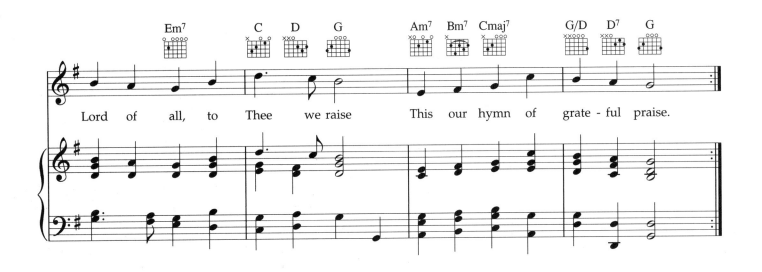

Lord of all, to Thee we raise This our hymn of grate-ful praise.

Verse 3:
For the joy of human love,
Brother, sister, parent, child,
Friends on earth, and friends above,
Pleasures pure and undefiled.
Lord of all, to Thee we raise
This our hymn of grateful praise.

Verse 4:
For each perfect gift of thine
To our race so freely given,
Graces human and divine,
Flowers of earth and buds of heaven.
Lord of all, to Thee we raise
This our hymn of grateful praise.

Verse 5:
For thy Church which evermore
Lifteth holy hands above,
Offering up on every shore
Her pure sacrifice of love.
Lord of all, to Thee we raise
This our hymn of grateful praise.

GLORIOUS THINGS OF THEE ARE SPOKEN

Words by John Newton
Music by Franz Joseph Haydn

A - ges found - ed, What can shake Thy sure re - pose?
such a ri - ver Ev - er flows their thirst to assuage?

With sal - va - tion's walls sur - round - ed,
Grace which, like the Lord, the Giv - er,

1. Thou mayst smile at all Thy foes.
2. Nev - er fails from age to age!

Verse 3:
Round each habitation hovering,
See the cloud and fire appear
For a glory and a covering,
Showing that the Lord is near.
Thus they march, their pillar leading,
Light by night, and shade by day;
Daily on the manna feeding
Which He gives them when they pray.

GUIDE ME, O THOU GREAT REDEEMER

Words by William Williams
Music by John Hughes

With strength ♩ = 94

CWM RHONDDA

1. Guide me, O Thou great Re-deem-er, Pil-grim through this bar-ren land; I am weak, but Thou art migh-ty; Hold me with Thy pow'r-ful hand; Bread of hea-ven,

2. O-pen now the cry-stal foun-tain, Whence the heal-ing stream doth flow; Let the fire and cloud-y pil-lar Lead me all my jour-ney through; Strong De-liv-erer,

with pedal

cresc. poco a poco

Verse 3:
When I tread the verge of Jordan,
Bid my anxious fears subside;
Death of death, and Hell's destruction,
Land me safe on Canaan's side;
Songs of praises, songs of praises,
I will ever give to Thee,
I will ever give to Thee.

HOLY, HOLY, HOLY! LORD GOD ALMIGHTY

Words by Reginald Heber
Music by John Bacchus Dykes

Verse 3:
Holy, holy, holy! Though the darkness hide Thee,
Though the sinful human eye Thy glory may not see,
Only Thou art holy; there is none beside Thee,
Perfect in power, in love, and purity.

Verse 4:
Holy, holy, holy! Lord God Almighty!
All Thy works shall praise Thy Name, in earth, and sky, and sea;
Holy, holy, holy! Merciful and mighty,
God in three Persons, blessed Trinity.

GLORY BE TO JESUS

English translation by Edward Caswall
Music by Friedrich Filitz

Worshipfully ♩ = 100

CASWALL

1. Glo - ry be to Je - sus,
3. Blest through end - less a - ges

(Verse 5 see block lyrics)

who in bit - ter pains
be the pre - cious stream,

poured for me the
which from end - less

life - blood from His sac - red veins!
tor - ment doth the world re - deem!

2. Grace and life e -
4. There the faint - ing
(Verses 6 and 7 see block lyrics)

dolce

-ter - nal in that blood I find,
spi - rit drinks of life her fill;

blest be His com -
there, as in a

**Repeat twice,
then D.S. al Fine**

-pas - sion, in - fi - nite - ly kind!
foun - tain, laves her - self at will.

8. Lift ye then your voi - ces; swell the migh - ty flood;

loud - er still and loud - er, praise the prec - ious blood.

Verse 5:
Abel's blood for vengeance
Pleaded to the skies;
But the blood of Jesus
For our pardon cries.

Verse 6:
Oft as it is sprinkled
On our guilty hearts,
Satan in confusion,
Terror-struck departs.

Verse 7:
Oft as earth exulting
Wafts its praise on high,
Angel hosts, rejoicing,
Make their glad reply.

JESU, LOVER OF MY SOUL

Words by Charles Wesley
Music by Joseph Parry

ABERYSTWYTH

Verse 3:
Thou, O Christ, art all I want;
More than all in Thee I find;
Raise the fallen, cheer the faint,
Heal the sick, and lead the blind.
Just and holy is Thy Name;
I am all unrighteousness;
False and full of sin I am;
Thou art full of truth and grace.

Verse 4:
Plenteous grace with Thee is found,
Grace to cover all my sin;
Let the healing streams abound,
Make and keep me pure within.
Thou of life the fountain art,
Freely let me take of Thee:
Spring Thou up within my heart,
Rise to all eternity.

I CANNOT TELL

Traditional Irish
Words by William Y. Fullerton

LONDONDERRY AIR

1. I can-not tell how he whom an-gels wor-ship should stoop to
(Verses 2 and 3 see block lyrics)

love the peo-ples of the earth, or why as

shep - herd he should seek the wand_ 'rer with his_ mys_ te - rious pro-mise of new

Verse 2:
I cannot tell how silently he suffered,
As with his peace he graced this place of tears,
Or how his heart upon the cross was broken,
The crown of pain to three and thirty years.
But this I know, he heals the broken-hearted,
And stays our sin, and calms our lurking fear,
And lifts the burden from the heavy-laden,
For yet the Saviour, Saviour of the world is here.

Verse 3:
I cannot tell how he will win the nations,
How he will claim his earthly heritage,
How satisfy the needs and aspirations
Of East and West, of sinner and of sage.
But this I know, all flesh shall see his glory,
And he shall reap the harvest he has sown,
And some glad day his sun shall shine in splendour
When he the Saviour, Saviour of the world is known.

IMMORTAL, INVISIBLE, GOD ONLY WISE

Words by Walter C. Smith
Music by John Roberts

SAINT DENIO

Verse 3:
To all life Thou givest, to both great and small;
In all life Thou livest, the true life of all;
We blossom and flourish, like leaves on the tree,
Then wither and perish; but nought changeth thee.

Verse 4:
Great Father of glory, pure Father of light,
Thine angels adore Thee, all veiling their sight;
All laud we would render: O help us to see
'Tis only the splendour of light hideth Thee.

JESUS CHRIST IS RISEN TODAY

Traditional

EASTER HYMN

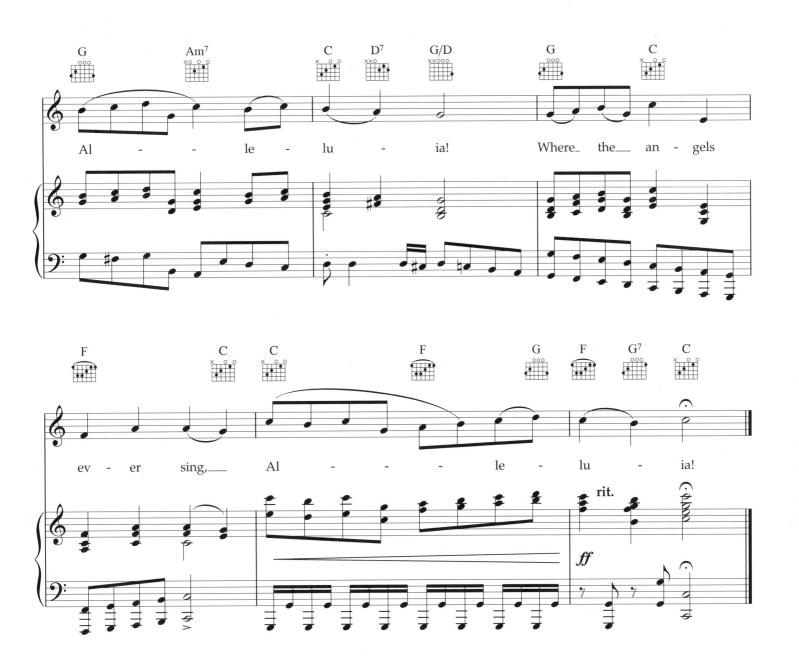

Verse 3:
But the pains that He endured, Alleluia!
Our salvation have procured, Alleluia!
Now above the sky He's King, Alleluia!
Where the angels ever sing, Alleluiah!

JESUS, GOOD ABOVE ALL OTHER

Traditional
Words by Percy Dearmer

QUEM PASTORES

Smooth and flowing ♩ = 100

1. Je - sus, good a - bove___ all oth - er,
2. Je - sus, cra - dled in___ a man - ger,

(Verses 3 and 4 see block lyrics)

mp

Con Ped.

gen - tle Child___ of gen - tle Moth - er,
for___ us fa - cing ev - 'ry dan - ger,

in a sta - ble born our Re - deem - er,
liv - ing as a home - less___ stran - ger,

Verse 3:

Jesus, for Thy people dying,
Risen Master, death defying,
Lord in heaven, Thy grace supplying,
Keep us to Thy presence near.

Verse 4:

Jesus, who our sorrows bearest,
All our thoughts and hopes Thou sharest,
Thou to man the truth declarest;
Help us all Thy truth to hear.

LEAD US, HEAVENLY FATHER, LEAD US

Words by James Edmeston
Music by Friedrich Filitz

MANNHEIM

Hopefully ♩ = 100

1. Lead us, heav'n-ly Fath - er, lead us
2. Sa - viour, breathe for - give - ness o'er us;

o'er the world's tem - pes - tuous sea; guard us, guide us,
all our weak - ness Thou dost know; Thou didst tread this

keep us, feed us, for we have no help but Thee;
earth be - fore us; Thou didst feel its keen - est woe;

yet pos - ses - sing ev - 'ry bless - ing, if our God our
yet un - fear - ing, per - se - ver - ing, to Thy pas - sion

Fath - er be.
Thou didst go.

3. Spi - rit of our God, des - cen - ding, fill our hearts with

mf cantabile

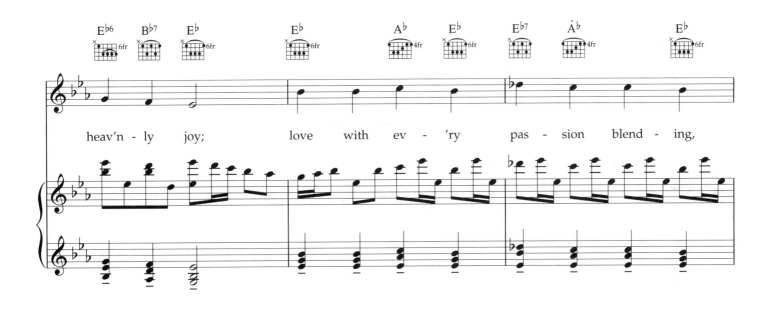

heav'n - ly joy; love with ev - 'ry pas - sion blend - ing,

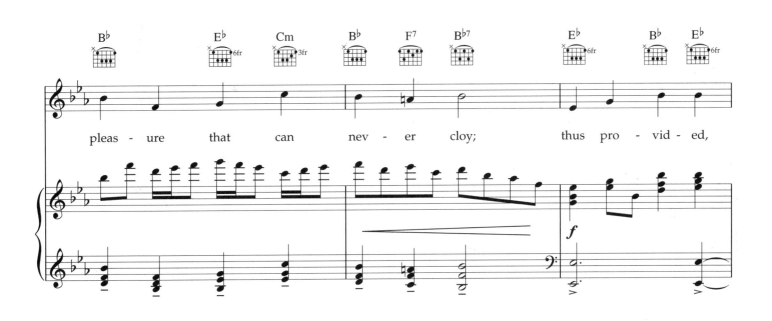

pleas - ure that can nev - er cloy; thus pro - vid - ed,

par - doned, gui - ded, noth - ing can our peace des - troy.

THE LORD IS MY SHEPHERD

Traditional
Music by Jessie Seymour Irvine

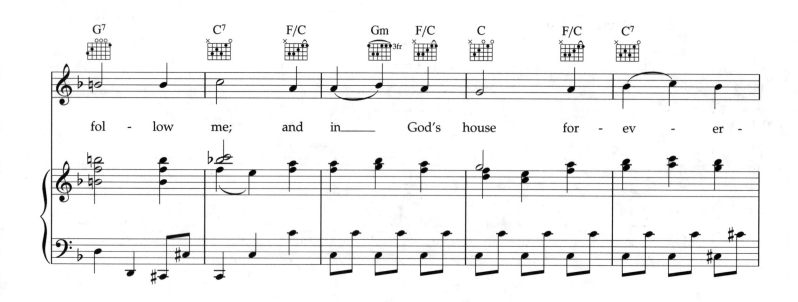

fol - low me; and in___ God's house for - ev - er -

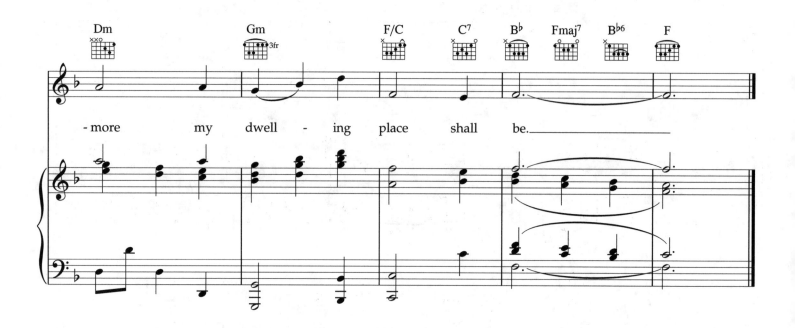

-more my dwell - ing place shall be._____

Verse 3:
Yea, though I walk in death's dark vale,
Yet will I fear no ill;
For Thou art with me; and Thy rod
And staff my comfort still.

Verse 4:
My table Thou hast furnished
In presence of my foes;
My head Thou dost with oil anoint,
And my cup overflows.

LOVE DIVINE, ALL LOVES EXCELLING

Words by Charles Wesley
Music by William P. Rowlands

BLAENWERN

1. Love div - ine, all loves ex - cel - ling, joy of heav'n, to earth come
2. Come, al - migh - ty to de - liv - er, let us all Thy life re -

(Verse 3 see block lyrics)

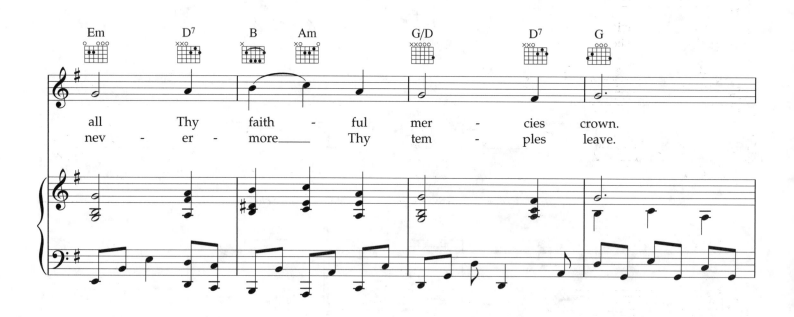

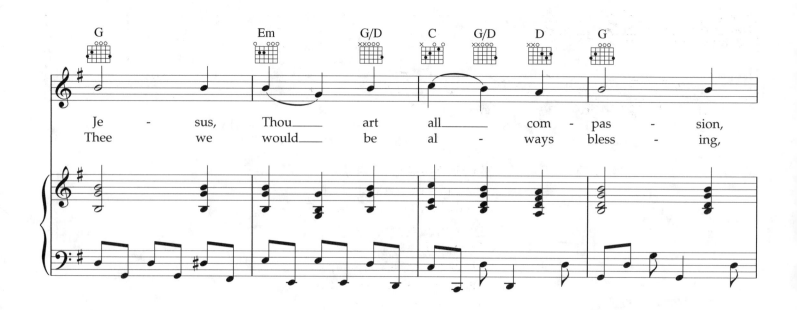

Verse 3:

Finish then Thy new creation;

Pure and spotless let us be;

Let us see Thy great salvation

Perfectly restored in Thee:

Changed from glory into glory,

Till in heaven we take our place,

Till we cast our crowns before Thee,

Lost in wonder, love and praise.

MY SONG IS LOVE UNKNOWN

Traditional
Words by Samuel Crossman

LOVE UNKNOWN

1. My song is love un -
2. He came from His un blest

(Verses 3-6 see block lyrics)

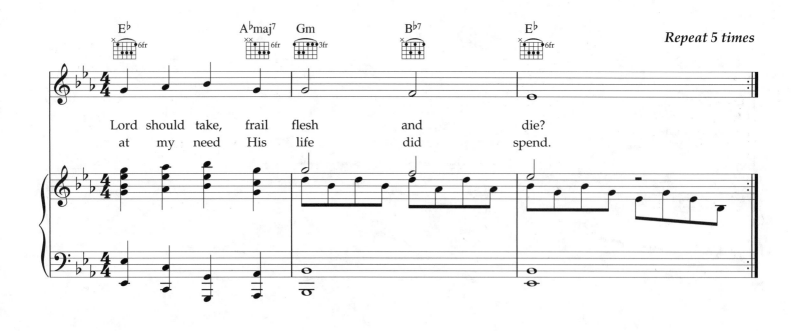

Lord should take, frail flesh and die?
at my need His life did spend.

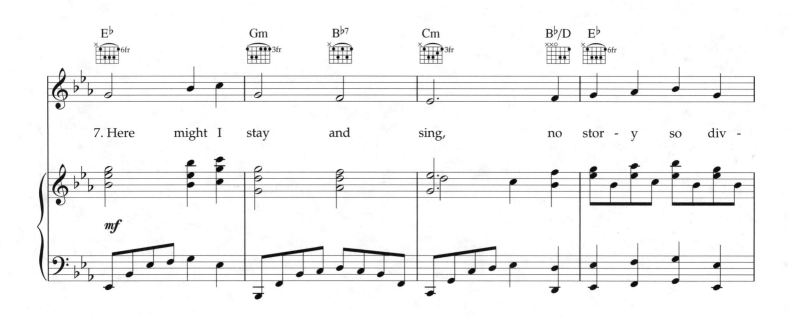

7. Here might I stay and sing, no stor - y so div -

- ine; nev - er was love, dear King! Nev - er was grief___ like

Verse 3:
Sometimes they strew His way,
And His sweet praises sing;
Resounding all the day
Hosannas to their King:
Then "Crucify!" is all their breath,
And for His death they thirst and cry.

Verse 4:
Why, what hath my Lord done?
What makes this rage and spite?
He made the lame to run,
He gave the blind their sight,
Sweet injuries! Yet they at these
Themselves displease, and 'gainst Him rise.

Verse 5:
They rise and needs will have
My dear Lord made away;
A murderer they saved,
The Prince of life they slay,
Yet cheerful He to suffering goes,
That He His foes from thence might free.

Verse 6:
In life, no house, no home
My Lord on earth might have;
In death no friendly tomb
But what a stranger gave.
What may I say? Heav'n was His home;
But mine the tomb wherein He lay.

NEARER, MY GOD, TO THEE

Words by Sarah F. Adams
Music by Lowell Mason

Verse 3:
There let the way appear, steps unto heav'n;
All that Thou sendest me, in mercy given;
Angels to beckon me nearer, my God, to Thee.

Refrain:
Nearer, my God, to Thee,
Nearer to Thee!

Verse 4:
Then, with my waking thoughts bright with Thy praise,
Out of my stony griefs Bethel I'll raise;
So by my woes to be nearer, my God, to Thee.
(Refrain)

Verse 5:
Or, if on joyful wing cleaving the sky,
Sun, moon, and stars forgot, upward I'll fly,
Still all my song shall be, nearer, my God, to Thee.
(Refrain)

NOW THANK WE ALL OUR GOD

Words and Music by Geoffrey Shaw, Martin Rinkart and Johann Crueger

NUN DANKET

With grandeur ♩ = 100

1. Now thank we all our
may this boun - teous
(Verse 3 see block lyrics)

God, with heart and hands and voic - es, who
God through all our life be near us, with

Verse 3:
All praise and thanks to God
The Father now be given,
The Son, and Holy Ghost,
Supreme in highest heaven,
The one eternal God,
Whom earth and heaven adore;
For thus it was, is now,
And shall be evermore.

O, FOR A CLOSER WALK WITH GOD

Traditional
Words by William Cowper

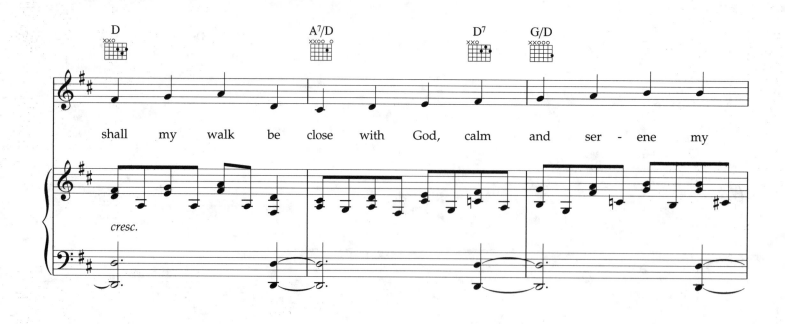

shall my walk be close with God, calm and ser - ene my

frame; so pur - er light shall mark the road that

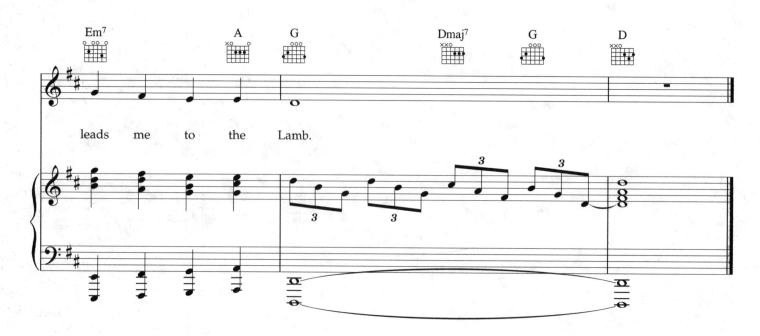

leads me to the Lamb.

O GOD, OUR HELP IN AGES PAST

Words by Isaac Watts
Music by William Croft

SAINT ANNE

Verse 3:
Before the hills in order stood,
Or earth received her frame,
From everlasting Thou art God,
To endless years the same.

Verse 4:
A thousand ages in Thy sight
Are like an evening gone;
Short as the watch that ends the night
Before the rising sun.

Verse 5:
Time, like an ever-rolling stream,
Bears all its sons away;
They fly, forgotten, as a dream
Dies at the opening day.

O PRAISE YE THE LORD!

Words by Henry Williams Baker
Music by Hubert H. Parry

LAUDATE DOMINUM

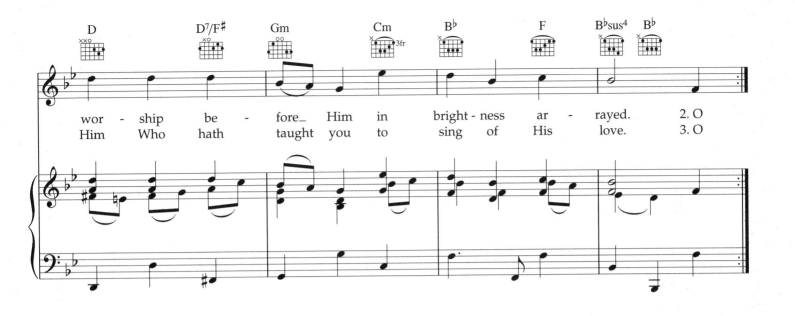

wor - ship be - fore_ Him in bright - ness ar - rayed. 2. O
Him Who be hath taught you to sing of His love. 3. O

right. 8. For this is His Word: His saints shall not

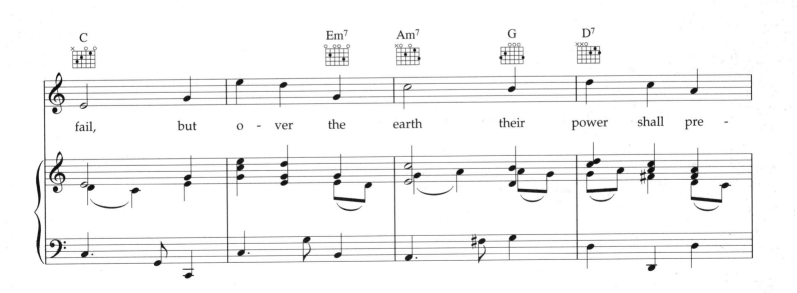

fail, but o - ver the earth their power shall pre -

vail; all king-doms and na-tions__ shall__ yield to their

sway. To God give the glor-y and praise Him for aye.

Verse 3:

O praise ye the Lord! All things that give sound;
Each jubilant chord re-echo around;
Loud organs, His glory forth tell in deep tone,
And sweet harp, the story of what He hath done.

Verse 4:

O praise ye the Lord! Thanksgiving and song
To Him be outpoured all ages along!
For love in creation, for Heaven restored,
For grace of salvation, O praise ye the Lord!

Verse 5:

O praise ye the Lord and sing a new song,
Amid all His saints His praises prolong;
The praise of their Maker His people shall sing,
And children of Zion rejoice in their King.

Verse 6:

With timbrel and harp and joyful acclaim,
With gladness and mirth, sing praise to His Name,
For God in His people His pleasure doth seek,
With robes of salvation He clotheth the meek.

Verse 7:

In glory exult, ye saints of the Lord;
With songs in the night, high praises accord;
Go forth in His service, be strong in His might,
To conquer all evil and stand for the right.

ONWARD, CHRISTIAN SOLDIERS

Words by Sabine Baring-Gould
Music by Arthur Sullivan

With confidence ♩ = 120

SAINT GERTRUDE

1. On - ward, Christ-ian sol - diers, march-ing as to war,
2. At the sign of tri - umph Sa - tan's host doth flee;

(Verses 3-6 see block lyrics)

with the cross of Je - sus go - ing on be - fore!
on then, Christ - ian sol - diers, on to vic - tor - y!

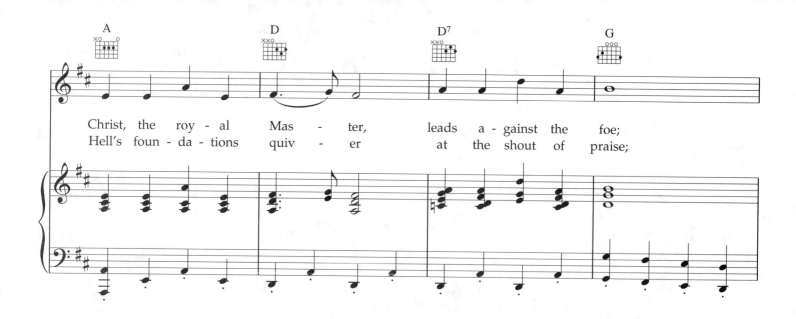

Christ, the roy - al Mas - ter, leads a - gainst the foe;
Hell's foun - da - tions quiv - er at the shout of praise;

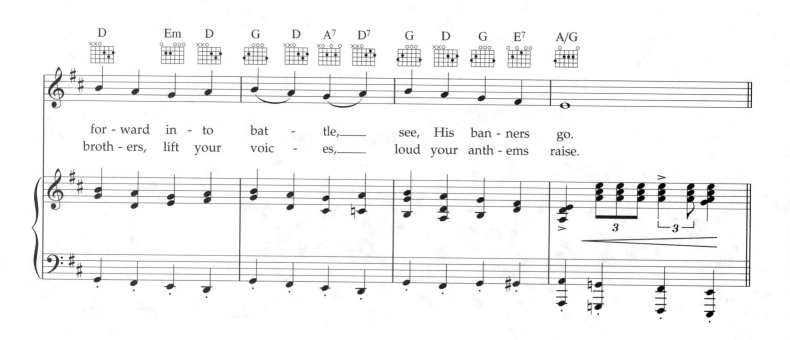

for - ward in - to bat - tle,___ see, His ban - ners go.
broth - ers, lift your voic - es,___ loud your anth - ems raise.

Refrain

On - ward, Christ - ian sol - diers,___ march - ing as to___ war,

Verse 3:
Like a mighty army
Moves the Church of God;
Brothers, we are treading
Where the saints have trod;
We are not divided,
All one body we,
One in hope and doctrine,
One in charity.
(Refrain)

Verse 5:
Crown and thrones may perish,
Kingdoms rise and wane,
But the Church of Jesus
Constant will remain;
Gates of hell can never
'Gainst that Church prevail;
We have Christ's own promise,
And that cannot fail.
(Refrain)

Verse 4:
What the saints established
That I hold for true.
What the saints believèd,
That I believe too.
Long as earth endureth,
Men the faith will hold,
Kingdoms, nations, empires,
In destruction rolled.
(Refrain)

Verse 6:
Onward, then, ye people,
Join our happy throng;
Blend with ours your voices
In the triumph song:
Glory, laud and honour
Unto Christ the King;
This through countless ages
Men and angels sing.
(Refrain)

PRAISE, MY SOUL, THE KING OF HEAVEN

Words by Henry F. Lyte
Music by John Goss

Majestically ♩ = 90
LAUDA ANIMA
D A7/E Dmaj7 G D Em7 Bm
Gmaj7 D Em9 Asus4 A D A7 Dmaj7
1. Praise, my soul, the King of
2. Praise Him for His grace and
(Verse 3 see block lyrics)
f
G D Em7 Bm Gmaj7 D Em9 Asus4 A
Heav - en; to his feet Thy trib - ute bring;
fa - vour to our fath - ers in dis - tress;

109

Verse 3:

Father-like, He tends and spares us;
Well our feeble frame He knows;
In His hand He gently bears us,
Rescues us from all our foes.
Alleluia, alleluia!
Widely yet His mercy flows.

PRAISE TO THE HOLIEST IN THE HEIGHT

Words by John Henry Newman
Music by John Bacchus Dykes

GERONTIUS

Joyfully ♩ = 106

1. Praise to the Ho - liest in the height,
2. O lov - ing wis - dom of our God!

(Verses 3-6 see block lyrics)

and in the depth be praise;
when all was sin be and shame,

in all His words most won - der - ful, most
a sec - ond Ad - am to the fight and

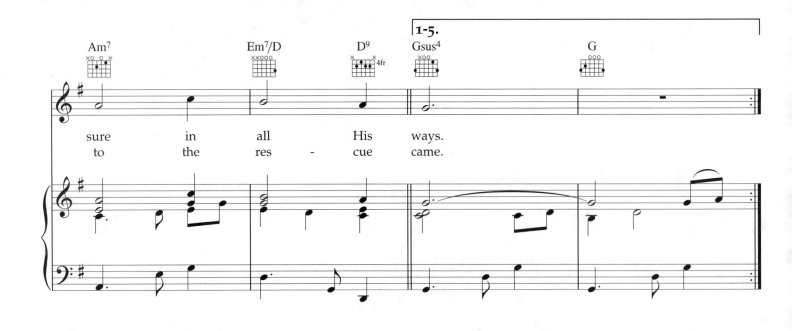

1-5.

sure   in   all   His   ways.
to   the   res - cue   came.

6.

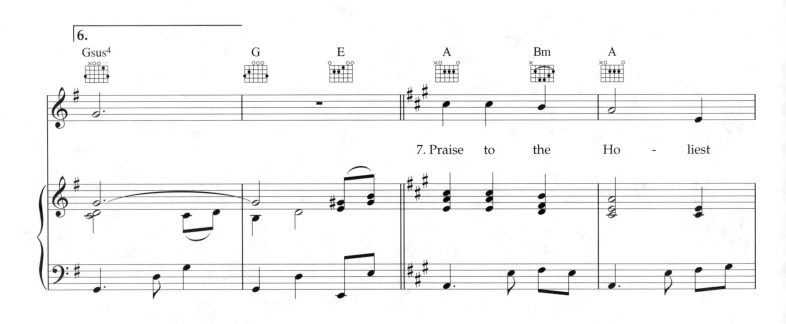

7. Praise   to   the   Ho - liest

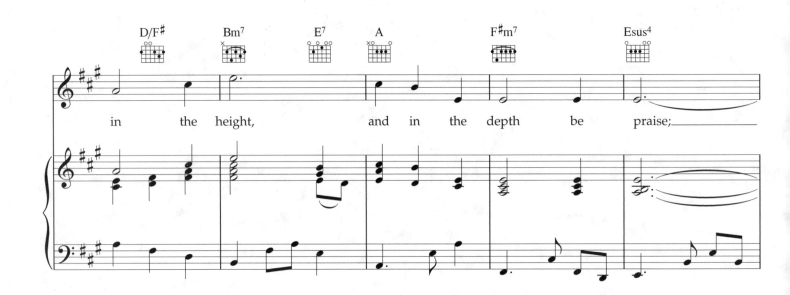

in   the   height,   and   in   the   depth   be   praise;

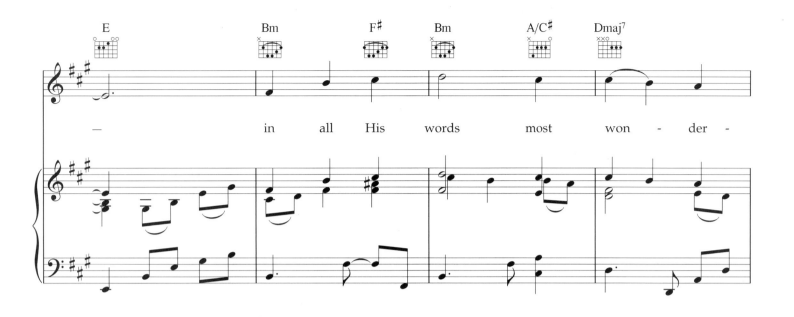

in all His words most won - der -

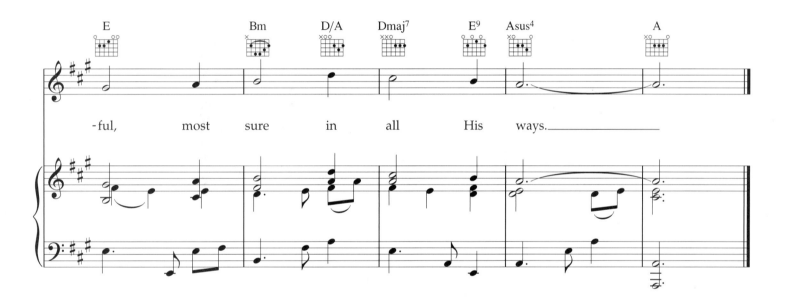

-ful, most sure in all His ways._____

Verse 3:
O wisest love! That flesh and blood,
Which did in Adam fail,
Should strive afresh against the foe,
Should strive and should prevail.

Verse 4:
And that a higher gift than grace
Should flesh and blood refine,
God's Presence and His very Self,
And Essence all-divine.

Verse 5:
O generous love! That He, who smote,
In Man for man the foe,
The double agony in Man
For man should undergo.

Verse 6:
And in the garden secretly,
And on the Cross on high,
Should teach His brethren, and inspire
To suffer and to die.

PRAISE TO THE LORD, THE ALMIGHTY

Traditional
Words by Joachim Neander and Catherine Winkworth

LOBE DEN HERREN

Verse 3:
Praise to the Lord,
Who doth prosper thy work and defend thee;
Surely His goodness and mercy shall daily attend thee.
Ponder anew what the Almighty can do,
If to the end He befriend thee.

REJOICE, THE LORD IS KING!

Words by Charles Wesley
Music by John Darwall

With strength and joy ♩ = 100

DARWALL'S 148TH

Verse 3:
His kingdom cannot fail;
He rules o'er earth and heaven;
The keys of death and hell
Are to our Jesus given.
Lift up your heart, lift up your voice!
Rejoice, again I say, rejoice!

Verse 4:
Rejoice in glorious hope!
Jesus the Judge shall come
And take his servants up
To their eternal home.
Lift up your heart, lift up your voice!
Rejoice, again I say, rejoice!

ROCK OF AGES

Words and Music by Augustus M. Toplady

With strength ♩ = 76

TOPLADY

Verse 3:
Nothing in my hands I bring,
Simply to the cross I cling;
Naked, come to Thee for dress;
Helpless look to Thee for grace;
Tainted, to the fountain fly;
Wash me, Saviour, or I die.

Verse 4:
While I draw this fleeting breath,
When mine eyelids close in death,
When I soar through tracts unknown
See Thee on Thy judgement throne,
Rock of Ages, cleft for me,
Let me hide myself in Thee.

STAND UP, STAND UP FOR JESUS

Words by George Duffield
Music by George J. Webb

Strong and march-like ♩ = 112

MORNING LIGHT

Verse 3:
Stand up, stand up, for Jesus;
Stand in his strength alone;
The arm of flesh will fail you,
Ye dare not trust your own:
Put on the Gospel armour,
And watching unto prayer,
When duty calls, or danger,
Be never wanting there.

Verse 4:
Stand up, stand up, for Jesus;
The strife will not be long:
This day, the noise of battle;
The next, the victor's song.
To him that overcometh
A crown of life shall be;
He with the King of glory
Shall reign eternally.

TAKE MY LIFE, AND LET IT BE

Words by Frances R. Havergal
Music by Wolfgang Amadeus Mozart

NOTTINGHAM

filled   with   mes - sa - ges   from   Thee.
e - v'ry   po - wer   as   Thou   shalt   choose.

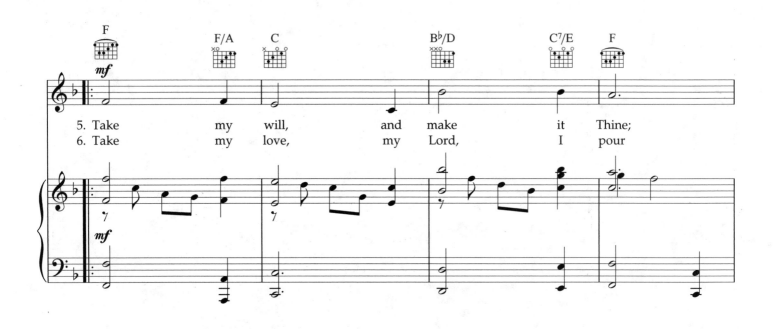

5. Take   my   will,   and   make   it   Thine;
6. Take   my   love,   my   Lord,   I   pour

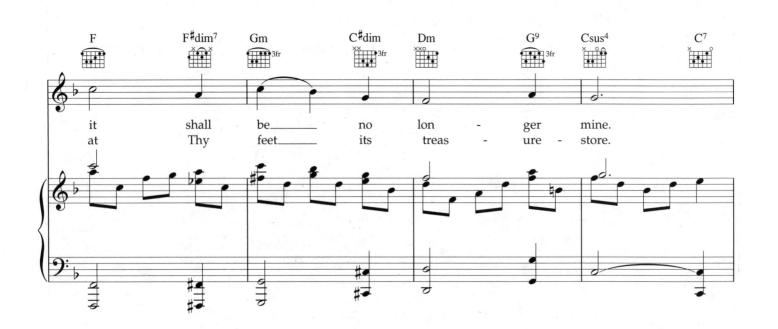

it   shall   be_____   no   lon - ger   mine.
at   Thy   feet_____   its   treas - ure - store.

Take my heart, it is Thine own; Take my-self, and I will be

1.

it shall be____ Thy roy - al throne.
ev - er, on - ly, all for

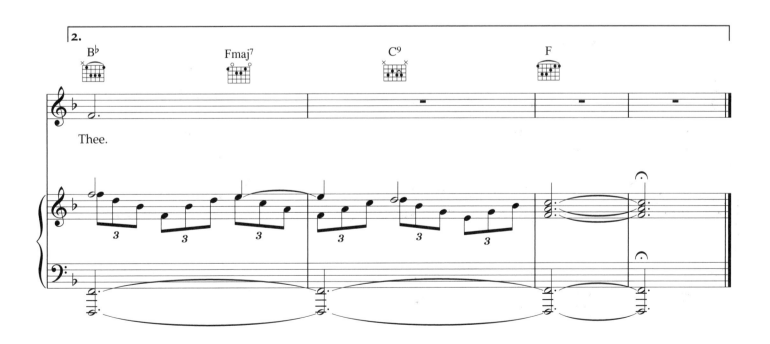

2.

Thee.

THERE IS A GREEN HILL FAR AWAY

Words by Cecil F. Alexander
Music by George C. Stebbins

HORSLEY

Verse 3:
He died that we might be forgiven,
He died to make us good,
That we might go at last to heaven,
Saved by His precious blood.

Verse 4:
There was no other good enough
To pay the price of sin,
He only could unlock the gate
Of heaven and let us in.

THINE BE THE GLORY

Words by Edmund Louis Budry and Richard Hoyle
Music by George Frideric Handel

MACCABAEUS

1.Thine be the glory, ris — en___ conqu-'ring Son;
2. Lo! Je - sus meets us, ris — en from the tomb;

(Verse 3 see block lyrics)

end - less___ is the vic - t'ry,
lov - ing - ly He greets us,

Thou o'er___ death hast won;
scat - ters___ fear and gloom;

an - gels___ in bright
let___ the church with

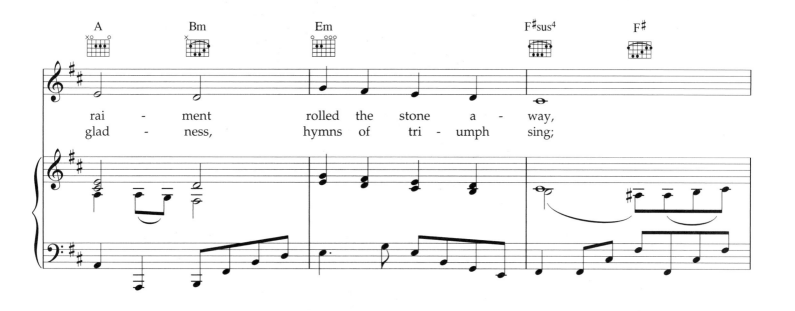

rai - ment   rolled the stone a - way,
glad - ness,   hymns of tri - umph sing;

kept_ the_ fold - ed grave - clothes   where Thy_ bo - dy
for_ her_ Lord now liv - eth,   death hath_ lost its

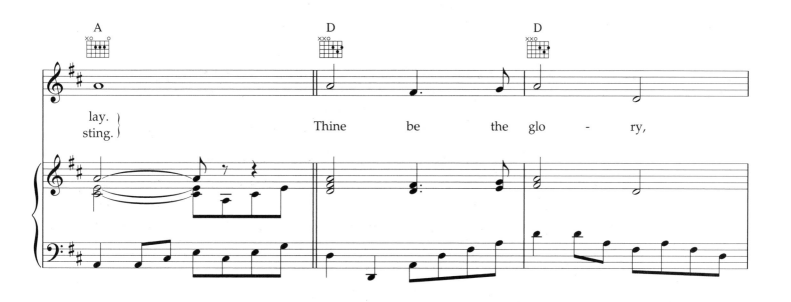

lay.
sting.   Thine be the glo - ry,

ris - en___ conqu' - ring Son, end - less___ is the

vic - t'ry Thou o'er___ death hast won. won.

Verse 3:

No more we doubt Thee, glorious Prince of Life;

Life is naught without Thee, aid us in our strife;

Make us more than conqu'rors, through Thy deathless love;

Bring us safe through Jordan to Thy home above.

Thine be the glory...

THY HAND, O GOD, HAS GUIDED

Words by Edward H. Plumptre
Music by Basil Harwood

fath - ers owned Thy good - ness, and we__ their deeds re -
this__ was all their teach - ing, in ev - 'ry deed and

cord; and both of__ this bear wit - ness, "One
word; to both all a - like pro - claim - ing, "One

Church, one Faith, one Lord."
Church, one Faith, one Lord."

2. Thy
3. When

134

Church, one Faith, one Lord."

rit.

Verse 3:
When shadows thick were falling,
And all seemed sunk in night,
Thou, Lord, didst send Thy servants
Thy chosen sons of light.
On them and on Thy people
Thy plenteous grace was poured,
And this was still their message:
"One Church, one Faith, one Lord."

Verse 4:
Through many a day of darkness,
Through many a scene of strife,
The faithful few fought bravely,
To guard the nation's life.
Their Gospel of redemption,
Sin pardoned, hope restored,
Was all in this enfolded,
"One Church, one Faith, one Lord."

Verse 5:
And we, shall we be faithless?
Shall hearts fail, hands hang down?
Shall we evade the conflict,
And cast away our crown?
Not so: in God's deep counsels
Some better thing is stored:
We will maintain, unflinching,
"One Church, one Faith, one Lord."

Verse 6:
Thy mercy will not fail us,
Nor leave Thy work undone,
With Thy right hand to help us,
The victory shall be won;
And then, by men and angels,
Thy Name shall be adored,
And this shall be their anthem,
"One Church, one Faith, one Lord."

TO GOD BE THE GLORY!

Words by Fanny J. Crosby
Music by William H. Doane

Verse 3:
Great things He hath taught us, great things He hath done,
And great our rejoicing through Jesus the Son;
But purer, and higher, and greater will be
Our wonder, our transport, when Jesus we see.

WE PLOUGH THE FIELDS AND SCATTER

Words by Matthias Claudius
Music by Johann Schulz

WIR PFLÜGEN

all things bright and good, the seed time and the har - vest, our

life, our health, our food; no gifts have we to of - fer for

all Thy love im - parts, and, what Thou most de - sir - est: our

hum - ble, thank - ful hearts.

D.S. al Coda

Coda

love.

WHAT A FRIEND WE HAVE IN JESUS

Words by Joseph Scriven
Music by Charles Converse

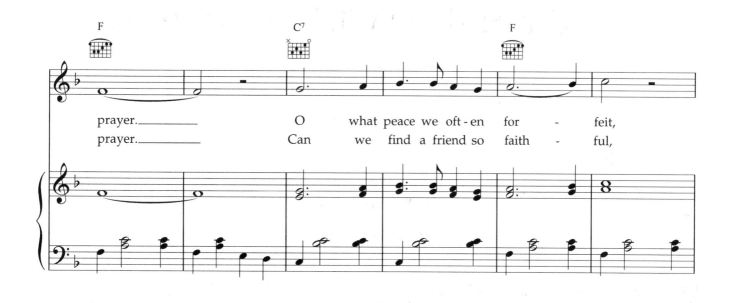

prayer._____ O what peace we oft-en for - feit,
prayer._____ Can we find a friend so faith - ful,

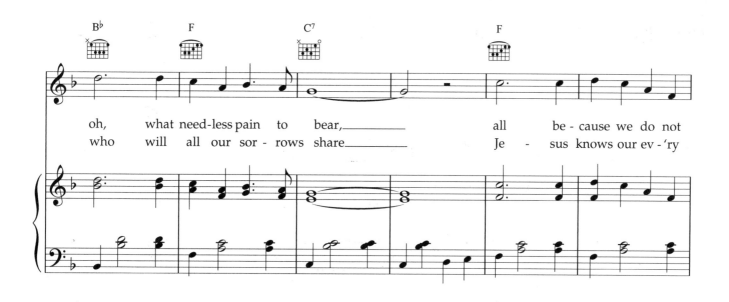

oh, what need-less pain to bear,_____ all be - cause we do not
who will all our sor - rows share_____ Je - sus knows our ev -'ry

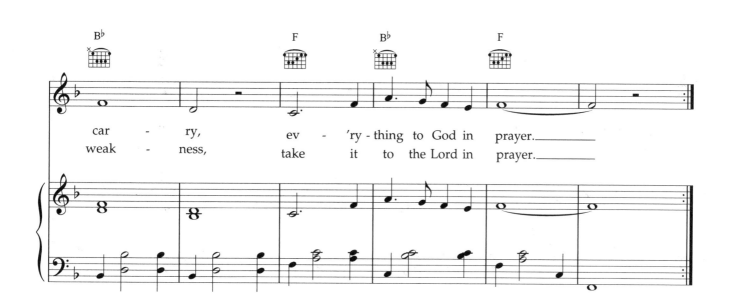

car - ry, ev - 'ry-thing to God in prayer._____
weak - ness, take it to the Lord in prayer._____

123456789

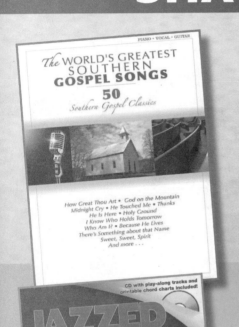
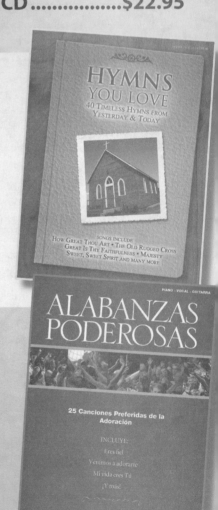